Channeling Matriarchs

poems by

Lynn Aprill

Finishing Line Press
Georgetown, Kentucky

Channeling Matriarchs

Copyright © 2021 by Lynn Aprill
ISBN 978-1-64662-573-4 First Edition
All rights reserved under International and Pan-American Copyright Conventions. No part of this book may be reproduced in any manner whatsoever without written permission from the publisher, except in the case of brief quotations embodied in critical articles and reviews.

ACKNOWLEDGMENTS

"The Fruit of the Tree" was first published in *Quartet* poetry journal's Summer 2021 issue.

"Sacrifice" is a found poem in blank verse influenced by *The Harlot by the Side of the Road* by Jonathan Kirsch.

"Reversal of Fortune" received Honorable Mention for poetry at the 14th Annual UW-Madison Writers Institute.

I would like to sincerely thank Ally—visual artist, former student, and current Curator of Public Programs at Museum of Wisconsin Art—for her beautiful depiction of the matriarchs.

Publisher: Leah Huete de Maines
Editor: Christen Kincaid
Cover Art: Alexandria Wilber, "Channeling Matriarchs"
Author Photo: Emily Hodkiewicz
Cover Design: Elizabeth Maines McCleavy

Order online: www.finishinglinepress.com
also available on amazon.com

Author inquiries and mail orders:
Finishing Line Press
PO Box 1626
Georgetown, Kentucky 40324
USA

Table of Contents

Forward xi

The Fruit of the Tree 1

Discovery 2

Salt 3

Captivating 4

Affliction 6

Vindicated 7

Wander 9

Harlot No More 11

Revolution 12

Sacrifice 13

Trust 15

Bitter and Blessed 16

Give and Take 17

Abigail's Arithmetic 19

Lamentations 20

Reversal of Fortune 22

Matriarch 23

Notes 24

*For Ruth, Vera, Adella and all of the matriarchs
who have gone before me;
And for Ben and Marissa, who allowed me to join their company.*

*"Bless the largeness in me, even when I fear it.
When I am dust, sing these words over my bones... she was a voice."
Sue Monk Kidd*

Forward

Three books which have significantly changed my perspective on my faith are *Genesis: A Living Conversation* by Bill Moyers, *The Harlot by the Side of the Road* by Jonathan Kirsch, and *The Red Tent* by Anita Diamant. I began to wonder where the women fit into these Biblical narratives—there are too many times when they are silent. What was faith to these women? How did they come to be so casually sacrificed by their fathers, husbands, brothers? What can we learn from the matriarchs today? If the Bible had not been written from an entirely patriarchal point of view, what would these women have to say about their situations and their God? My hope is that these poems will stir the imagination with regard to these exceptional women whose stories shaped the future for our entire gender.

The Fruit of the Tree

> *"When the woman saw that the fruit of the tree was good for food and pleasing to the eye, and also desirable for gaining wisdom, she took some and ate it. She also gave some to her husband, who was with her, and he ate it."*
> *Genesis 3:6*

To be clear, I was not hungry,
not in the way that you think.
Yes, the fruit was ripe and red and enticing,
but for all that, it wasn't the fruit—

it was the knowledge.
Every trip through the garden, encountering
fantastical animals and abundant vegetation, I'd say,
"This is Breeze Floater," only to be told, "No,
that is a fern," or "That is Tree Eater," and hear,
"I named it woodchuck." To walk
through my own world and not name it
was more than I could bear.

So when the snake said
"Knowledge," the fruit was in my mouth
before he hissed another word. In that moment,
I knew it all—every living thing, every story.

The first sin wasn't disobedience,
it was envy. Or superciliousness, depending
on which gender you want to blame.
My struggle with sin was not in taking the fruit—
it was in sharing knowledge with him
because for two seconds
I was the first to know.

Discovery

> *"To the woman [God] said, 'I will make your pains in childbearing very severe; with painful labor you will give birth to children.'"*
> *"Adam lay with his wife Eve, and she became pregnant and gave birth to Cain. She said 'With the help of the Lord I have brought forth a man.' Later she gave birth to his brother Abel."*
> *Genesis 3:16 and 4:1-2*

It began and ended with blood.

I remembered what He had said
about the pain.
And there was that,
oh, yes, greatly multiplied,
and here was pain again
as bookends to Abel's existence.

But the blood which bloomed
like ripe apples in my palms
as I cradled my man child
perplexed me, even as the ground
opened its mouth to receive
this first warm offering.
In birth and in death
it drank his blood
and was still.

And Lucifer laughed in the land of Nod.

Salt

> *"But [Lot's] wife looked back from behind him, and she became a pillar of salt."*
> *Genesis 19:26*

Judgment is found
in fifteen words.
Blame finds me influencing
the choice of land in Jordan,
Shame is heaped upon my head
for faithless daughters
who married Sodomites,
Guilt is laid at my door
because my daughters—
fearing Armageddon—
gave birth to their own brothers.
History has me looking back,
longing for my home—
I turned back
to confront the face
of my husband's God.

Captivating

> "Isaac brought [Rebekah] into the tent of his mother Sarah, and he married Rebekah. So she became his wife, and he loved her; and Isaac was comforted after his mother's death."
> Genesis 24: 67

I was the watcher at the well,
waiting for you,
my poor, damaged Isaac.
Favorite of your mother,
who forced your father to turn
your own near-brother
into the wilderness
with a skin of water
and a promise of protection.

A father who was so anxious
to prove his obedience
that God had to call him twice—
Abraham. ABRAHAM!—
before he took the knife
from your throat
and turned it on
the sacrificial lamb.

I was the one God sent
to hold you in the night
when you felt the knife
again and again.

I was the one who carried
your two nations—already at war—
in my womb, along with the promise
that the older would serve the younger.

I was the one who loved you well.
Until . . .

Until I pulled the wool
over your weak eyes
with my own sacrificial lamb,
and you found yourself back on the altar.

Affliction

> "Now Laban had two daughters; the name of the older was Leah, and the name of the younger was Rachel. Leah had weak eyes, but Rachel was lovely in form, and beautiful."
> Genesis 29: 16-17

The Word says
my eyes were weak—
I say Jacob's eyes were weak
for they did not see
    that my hands were swift and sure,
    that my body was strong
    that I labored effortlessly.
They saw only
that Rachel was beautiful,
a lovely desert flower.

They did not see
    the household run by my hand,
    the weaving done by my word,
    the harvest reaped by my command.
They saw only
that Rachel was beautiful,
a lotus in the wilderness.

But they could not ignore
six strong sons
to follow their father
and their father's God.
Then Jacob's eyes cleared,
and Rachel wept,
a well of sorrow in Nahor.

Vindicated

> "Now Dinah, the daughter Leah had borne to Jacob, went out to visit the women of the land... And Shechem said to his father Hamor, 'Get me this girl as my wife.'"
> Genesis 34: 1 and 4

In a house running high to sons,
I grew up, the only daughter,
precious to all my mothers,
a pawn in the eyes of my father,
a piece to be put into play
to gain the best position
in this land of Canaan.

Do you wonder at my gambit,
to escape my canvas prison
and seek solace in the daughters of the land?
Instead, I found a prince,
tall and sure, so unlike
my bandy-legged brothers
with their slings and arrows.

Captured by his charm,
did I go willingly to my defilement?
Did I invite his advances
and defy my father's strictures?
To keep me in check,
my birth brothers, Simeon and Levi,
demanded an outlandish sacrifice—
the wholesale circumcision of every male—
then dragged me screaming from his bed
after they'd slit his throat.

And there my story ends.
Except...

With his last breath,
my father judged my brothers
and banished their offspring
to the edges of Israel.

Checkmate.

Wander

> "Then his sister asked Pharaoh's daughter, 'Shall I go and get one of the Hebrew women to nurse the baby for you?' 'Yes, go,' she answered. So the girl went and got the baby's mother."
> Exodus 2: 7-8

Prophet protector,
bullrush watcher,
leader of women
and singer of songs.
I made my mother
a wetnurse to her own son.
I watched from afar
as Moses rose in Pharaoh's house,
cherished surrogate son.

At Israel's deliverance,
I watched the waters close
over Pharaoh's hoard
and led the women
in the national anthem
of our newborn Israel:
"Sing ye to the Lord,
for He hath triumphed gloriously!"

But pride goeth before a fall,
and soon I was murmuring against Moses,
bitter that my younger brother had God's ear.
Bitter also that he took to wife
a Cushite, an unbeliever.
Our ironic God dealt me
a fitting punishment—
for speaking against one black as night,
He turned me white as snow,
an outcast from my people
for seven long, leprous days.

My spirit healed, I met my end
on the very brink of the Promised Land,
destined to die in the wilderness.

Harlot No More

> *"And Joshua sent . . . two men to spy secretly, saying 'Go view the land, even Jericho.' And they went, and came into an harlot's house, named Rahab, and lodged there . . . for her house was upon the town wall, and she dwelt upon the wall."*
> Joshua 2:1-15

Cast from my father's house
as a ruined woman,
a dweller of walls,
a keeper of secret things,
is it a wonder that God knew
where to send His men?
Who would question their presence
in the house of Rahab the Harlot?

Hidden in flax, my faith
was a secret shared with strangers
who bought my silence
with a scarlet rope.

On the Lord's day,
I hung blood in my window
and saved my soul.

They will have to rewrite my story
free of appositives.

Revolution

> "Blessed above women shall Jael, the wife of Heber the Kenite
> be, blessed shall she be above women in the tent."
> Judges 5:24

It was a cycle with these people
these Israelites, distant kin.
A generation, seldom more,
of adherence to their one God.
Then, fractious, stiff-necked people,
they would turn their faces
from their God, and He,
in turn, would allow them to be conquered.

So they made war on Jabin, King of Canaan,
and Sisera, captain of his army,
to free themselves from bondage.
Deborah and Barak, with ten thousand men—
Why tell you the story? It was not my fight!

And yet, I have my place in it,
for when Sisera fled the field
and sought shelter and succor in my tent,
the God of Israel showed me
the tent peg and the hammer
and the exact spot on Sisera's temple
to use them both.

And the children of Israel praised me
and lived in peace with their God . . .
for a time.

Sacrifice

> *"And it was a custom in Israel, that the daughters of Israel went yearly to lament the daughter of Jephthah the Gileadite four days in a year."*
> Judges 11:39-40

And when the Chosen people of God had
angered Jehovah once again, they begged
the mercenary Jephthah to save them
from the invading Ammonite army.
So Jephthah abandoned his only child.

> In his absence, his daughter passed beyond
> the little courtyard of their house, beyond
> the silent well in the town square, beyond
> the low gates on the outskirts of Mizpah.

And Jephthah made a vow unto the Lord—
"Make me victorious in battle, and
I will make sacrifice the very first
that greets me upon my returning home—
Yea, even as a burnt off'ring to you."

> Up and up, into the dusty hills
> where a spring bubbled up and an old oak
> did spread its branches, to that hidden place
> in the hills she returned once and again,
> in the company of young women whom
> she counted as worthy to know her heart.

Jephthah returned with the Lord's victory.
His daughter burst in welcome from the house,
and Jephthah crumpled into the dust, beat
his breast, rent his clothes and cried in anguish,
"My daughter, you have brought with you your Death!"

At his distress, his faithful daughter bade,
"So do to me what you have vowed to do . . .
Give me and my companions two months' time
to dwell apart and mourn what is to come."

> With her true friends, his daughter passed beyond
> the silent courtyard of their house, beyond
> the yawning well in the town square, beyond
> the lonely gates on the outskirts of town.

What grief did Jephthah know those two long months,
what tears fell on the rough altar of stone
which he did fashion in preparation
is only known between himself and God.

> Up and up, into the flowering hills
> the virgins climbed, sheltering near the oak
> which spread its branches. In that hidden place,
> in the company of young women whom
> she counted as worthy to touch her soul,
> did Jephtha's daughter spend her final days.

She did not struggle against the harsh blade
which took her, Virgin, still untouched by man.

Trust

> *"Naomi said, 'Return home, my daughters. Why would you come with me?'*
> *... But Ruth replied, 'Don't urge me to leave you or to turn back from you. Where you go I will go, and where you stay I will stay. Your people will be my people and your God my God.'"*
> *Ruth 1:11 and 16*

Mother-in-law. Such a strange term,
that, in-law. What law exists
which binds us together
even after the deaths of our men?
The law of my heart,
which opened to you
when I wed your son.
The law of my life,
which learned from you daily
as we laughed and toiled together,
building a home.
The law of my spirit,
which knit to yours
in the small hours of the morning
as the moon whispered
behind a line of sycamores,
and my husband's spirit took wing.
The law of my soul,
which would not be mended,
and yet was made whole again
by your quiet devotion to your God.

Even as bitterness took you from Moab,
I could not be parted from you,
Mother of my faith.

Lead . . . I follow.

Bitter and Blessed

> *"[Elkanah] had two wives, one was called Hannah and the other Peninnah. Peninnah had children, but Hannah had none."*
> *I Samuel 1:2*

Peninnah. A pearl. A treasure.
An open womb, that was Peninnah's worth.
She could give my husband sons,
while I had none,
but she could not capture his heart.
Instead she mocked my barrenness
while I wept and prayed,
fasted and wept. Then the Lord
heard the agony of my soul
and granted me a son,
on loan for three short years,
before I returned him to the temple.

Because I kept my bargain,
the Lord gifted me with more children—
three sons and two daughters—
and a yearly visit to my firstborn.
God has heard, my heart is full.

And Peninnah? She watches my children
through narrowed eyes. She has been weighed
and found wanting.

Give and Take

> *"Now Saul's daughter Michal was in love with David, and when they told Saul about it, he was pleased. "I will give her to him," he thought, "so that she may be a snare to him and so that the hand of the Philistines may be against him."*
> *I Samuel 18:20-21*

My father Saul was an arrogant
and rebellious man. Desperate
to retain his throne, he lived
by the dictum, "Keep your enemies close."
He was a grasper and a taker,
and I paid the price.

I watched from behind the curtain
as my sister was promised
to David, the chosen of the Lord.
My eyes shown with tears to think
that Merab would have him,
but Saul took her and gave her to another.
When David purchased my hand
with two hundred Philistine foreskins,
my father's heart burned with disappointment and rage.

Again and again, Saul sought David's life
with an ill-thrown spear, an assassin's blade,
until I helped him flee by filling his bed
with a graven image.

David traveled from kingdom to cave—
defeating Philistines,
conspiring with my brother,
moving his mother and father to safety in Moab—
with no thought of his wife.
Instead, he proposed—
to Abigail,
to Ahinoam,

to Maacah,
to Haggith,
to Abital,
to Eglah—
collecting wives and concubines
as he once collected foreskins,

while I was given to another,
a gentle man from the town of Gallim.

On the day David became king, he demanded
my return, so I journeyed to Jerusalem,
shadowed by my weeping husband.
There, I watched from the window
as my bridegroom leapt with abandon,
revealing himself to his people.

Weary of being taken
by one man and another,
I closed my heart,
and God closed my womb.

In the end, I raised Merab's five sons—
until my husband took them as well,
allowing them to be cut down
like so much wheat before the scythe.

Abigail's Arithmetic

> *"A certain man in Maon, who had property there at Carmel, was very wealthy... His name was Nabal and his wife's name was Abigail. She was an intelligent and beautiful woman.*
> *He is just like his name—his name is Fool, and folly goes with him."*
> I Samuel 25:2-25

I married Folly
and it cost me:

200 loaves
    2 skins of wine
    5 sheep (ready dressed)
    5 measures of grain (parched)
100 clusters of raisins
200 cakes of figs
    1 life, his (heart failure)

to correct his foolishness.

Lamentations

> "Rizpah . . . took sackcloth and spread it out for herself on a rock. From the beginning of the harvest till the rain poured down from the heavens on the bodies, she did not let the birds of the air touch them by day or the wild animals by night."
> 2 Samuel 21:10

I am Rizpah,
watcher of wolves and vultures—
Hear me, O Gibeon!

You hung my hopes
from the mountain tops
because God withheld
your rain—
Hear now my wrath
rain down upon your head!

You sacrificed my sons
for Saul's mistakes
and watered your fields
with my sorrow—
Hear me now, O great Gibeon!
May every tear
which falls upon your land
become thistle and thorn
to crown this king,
David, son of the fields!

I wrap my sons in sackcloth
and bury them with their father's bones
in the tomb of Kish.
My mouth is a furnace
filled with the ashes of the slain.
I bargain with beasts
to leave the bodies of
my sons undefiled.

Tell my tale, O Gibeon,
for I can speak
of nothing but death.

Reversal of Fortune

> *"If it pleases the king,"* [Queen Esther] said, *"and if he regards me with favor and thinks it the right thing to do, and if he is pleased with me, let an order be written overruling the dispatches that Haman . . . devised and wrote to destroy the Jews in all the king's provinces. For how can I bear to see disaster fall on my people? How can I bear to see the destruction of my family?"*
> Esther 8: 5-6

Haman, Haman,
with your ridiculous strut
and your ten slick sons,
did you think you would invent
genocide? Did you hope to destroy
all of the Chosen?
Did you call down
the king's wrath
and raise gallows
to hang your own generations upon?

Oh, foolish man
to think that God does not command
the consequences
of every cast of the lot.
More foolish yet
to throw yourself
upon the couch of a queen
and beg for pardon.

What can I do,
being only a woman,
and a Jew?

Matriarch

> *"Lo, children are an heritage of the LORD: and the fruit of the womb is his reward."*
> *Psalm 127:3*

And what of me?
For I, too, have been Matriarch
since the first day that I held you,
swaddled and safe,
secure as the firstborn—
destined to receive the practice,
not the polish,
recipient of the first draft,
the rough, harsh before,
never the smooth after.
And for that,

my heart weeps.
I'm sorry I struggled to find
      the strength of Leah,
      the bravery of Rahab,
      the faith of Ruth
      the fortitude of Hannah,
even as I stumbled my way
through matriarchy.

Just know, even now—
with my household
quietly childless—
you remain
my greatest gift.

Notes

The poems contained in *Channeling Matriarchs* are clearly fictional, and while I am in no way a Biblical scholar, the following notes may be of some assistance in understanding references in the preceding poems.

"Discovery" In Genesis, after Abel's murder (the first death recorded in the Bible), his brother and murderer Cain is banished by God to the Land of Nod, east of Eden. Nod is also Hebrew for "to wander," which may have indicated that Cain was banished to wander the earth.

"Salt" While the Christian Bible indeed only references Lot's wife with the fifteen words found in the quote from Genesis, the Jewish Midrash has much more to say of Lot's wife Edith (who is never named in the Christian Bible). In this further glimpse into the story, Edith refused to provide hospitality to the angels that visited her husband prior to the destruction of Sodom. Further, when asked to provide them with salt as was the custom, she grudgingly did so, but gossiped to the neighbors that her husband had guests, which caused the men of the town to storm the house, demanding Lot turn his guests over to be "used" by them. Instead, Lot offers the townsmen his daughters. Those same daughters, after the destruction of their home and the loss of their mother, knowing they alone escaped Sodom and fearing they were the last people on earth, decided to lay with their father to continue his family line.

"Captivating" Isaac's early life was, by turns, pampered and traumatic. Only son of his mother Sarah, Isaac was the second son of Abraham, who had first fathered Isaac's half-brother Ishmael with his slave Hagar (at his wife's request). Once Sarah had her own son, she forced Abraham to banish Ishmael and Hagar to the wilderness of Beersheba (after God had promised to take care of Ishmael and turn him into a great nation). Later, God asks Abraham to sacrifice Isaac to prove his devotion to God, calling on him to stop just before Abraham lowered the knife. Years later, after Isaac married Rebekah and fathered the twins Jacob and Esau, it is Rebekah this time who wounds him by tricking him into passing his blessing on to the younger twin Jacob (to fulfill God's prophecy that the older will serve the younger).

"Affliction" When Jacob went to his uncle Laban to seek a wife, he worked for seven years for the beautiful Rachel. Laban tricked Jacob at the wedding, and it was only afterwards that he realized he had married the wrong daughter—Leah. The Bible notes that Leah's eyes were weak, and that Jacob favored her sister Rachel and Rachel's children over Leah. In consolation, God granted her six sons and Jacob's only daughter Dinah. While Leah may not have been favored by her husband, I can't help but imagine that she turned her loneliness into the strength to run Jacob's household in spite of this.

"Vindicated" Whole books have been written about Jacob's sole daughter, Dinah (notably *The Red Tent* by Anita Diamant). While the Bible does not reveal much about her life nor her death, the one story we do hear is of her "defilement" by Shechem, the prince of the land in which her father dwelt. There is speculation about whether this was a case of rape, of consensual sex, of a misunderstanding between two cultures of what constituted "marriage"—regardless, when Shechem sends his father to ask Jacob and his sons to name the brideprice so he can officially marry Dinah, Jacob's sons instead ask for another offering—the circumcision of every man in the city. While the men are recovering, Jacob's sons Simeon and Levi go into the city and slit every man's throat, bringing Dinah back home. What becomes of Dinah afterwards is not revealed, but on his deathbed, Jacob curses Simeon and Levi's actions in this affair and grants them lands far separated from each other, to keep them from joining forces in this way again.

"Wander" Miriam, the sister of Moses, is first introduced to the Biblical reader when she helps her mother hide her baby brother in a basket in the Nile River after Pharoah has ordered the execution of all Israelite newborns. The rest of that story is well known (see *The Ten Commandments* with Charleton Heston!), but Miriam becomes a prophetess in her own right during the Exodus of the Israelites from Egypt. At one point (there are conflicting stories of the cause), Miriam speaks against Moses; as punishment, God afflicts her with leprosy for seven days.

"Harlot No More" Appositive = a phrase that renames the noun next to it. While some cultures credit Rahab with running or owning an inn, in the Christian tradition her name is synonymous with "harlot" or prostitute. When spies from Joshua come to scout Jericho before their invasion, they naturally stay with Rahab as no one would question her entertaining strange men. In return for her help, the men present her with a red rope to hang in her window; when Jericho falls, they will know where she is and save her.

"Revolution" Jael is a little-known figure in the Bible who, while not an Israelite, is a distant relative. She is credited with helping to end a battle with Canaan by murdering the captain of the Canaanite army who had sought refuge and rest in her tent. Instead, she drove a wooden tent peg through his head.

"Sacrifice" Jephthah is described variously as a judge and a mercenary. At the time of this story, he has agreed to lead the fight against the Ammonite army for Gilead in exchange for becoming their chieftain if successful. A faithful man, he prays for success in battle, vowing to sacrifice the first thing he sees upon returning home. That "thing" is, of course, his daughter cheering his success. While he regrets his vow, he is determined to follow through to thank God for his success. His daughter bargains two months to go into the mountains with her friends, and then she returns to become the sacrifice. Unlike Isaac, she was not spared at the last moment. As referenced in the text, some lines for this poem were borrowed from *The Harlot By the Side of the Road* by Jonathan Kirsch.

"Trust" There are probably few people who do not already know of the faith of Ruth, who followed her mother-in-law Naomi after both of their husbands had died, and trusts not only her mother-in-law but her God as well.

"Bitter and Blessed" Polygamy is certainly found repeatedly in the Old Testament. Hannah, the speaker in this poem, is the favored wife, but barren. Her husband marries again to Penninah, a fertile woman. The Bible describes Hannah weeping and praying to God for just one son, which she will dedicate back to Him. God grants her request in the form of the prophet Samuel, and she brings him back to the temple as soon as he is weaned. Because of her faith, she is then granted other children.

"Give and Take" Michal is one of the daughters of King Saul, first king of Israel. When it becomes clear that Saul is no longer favored by God and David has been anointed his successor, Saul goes to great lengths to defeat David. Saul envisions David's marriage to his daughter Michal as a trap for David, but Michal helps save David from her father on a number of occasions. In return, while David is on the run, he marries again and again. When he finally successfully becomes king, he insists on Michal's return as his wife, even though she has been married to another man for years. When Michal scorns David's celebration, she is punished with barrenness.

"Abigail's Arithmetic" Abigail becomes David's second wife, after her first husband (Nabal, which means "fool" in Hebrew) insulted David. Abigail bribes David with food to keep him from killing her foolish husband. Instead, God strikes him dead.

"Lamentations" Rizpah was one of Saul's concubines, having given him two sons. When a famine afflicts the land for three years, David is told that it is because of Saul and his offspring. Rizpah's two sons and Michal's five nephews were killed and hanged as a result. Rizpah then posts herself next to the bodies for five long months, chasing off birds and beasts, until David has them cut down and buried properly.

"Reversal of Fortune" Esther becomes Queen of Persia after King Ahasuerus' first wife refuses to obey him; unbeknownst to him, the beautiful new queen is also a Jew. When her cousin Mordecai angers Haman, the king's right-hand man, Haman receives permission to hunt down and kill all of the Jews in Persia. Queen Esther has to use all of her wit and courage to turn the tables on Haman and reveal to the King that Haman's plot would also mean her death. The gallows that Haman erected for Mordecai were later used on Haman and his sons.

Educator and writer **Lynn Aprill's** poems have appeared or are forthcoming in *Bramble*, Ambidextrous Bloodhound Press, Hip Circle Empowerment Center's International Women's Day *Choose To Challenge* Anthology, *WinglessDreamer*, *Quartet* journal, and Pure Slush's *Birth, Growing Up,* and *Love* volumes from the Lifespan project. A Wisconsin native, she received her Bachelor's degree in English from the University of Wisconsin-Eau Claire and her Master's degree in Curriculum and Instruction from the University of Wisconsin-Milwaukee. A classroom teacher for 27 years, Lynn received the Wisconsin Council of Teachers of English Chisholm Award for Meritorious Service to the Profession in 2012. She resides with her husband and various dogs on 40 acres in Northeast Wisconsin.

www.ingramcontent.com/pod-product-compliance
Lightning Source LLC
LaVergne TN
LVHW041506070426
835507LV00012B/1360